MENTAL HEALTH NCLEX-RN REVIEW:

100 Practice Questions with Detailed Rationales Explaining Correct & Incorrect Answer Choices

Disclaimer:

Although the author and publisher have made every effort to ensure that the information in this book was correct at press time, the author and publisher do not assume and hereby disclaim any liability to any party for any loss, damage, or disruption caused by errors or omissions, whether such errors or omissions result from negligence, accident, or any other cause.

This book is not intended as a substitute for the medical advice of physicians. The reader should regularly consult a physician in matters relating to their health and particularly with respect to any symptoms that may require diagnosis or medical attention.

All rights reserved. No part of this publication may be reproduced, distributed, or transmitted in any form or by any means, including photocopying, recording, or other electronic or mechanical methods, without the prior written permission of the publisher, except in the case of brief quotations embodied in critical reviews and certain other noncommercial uses permitted by copyright law.

NCLEX®, NCLEX®-RN, and NCLEX®-PN are registered trademarks of the National Council of State Boards of Nursing, Inc. They hold no affiliation with this product.

Some images within this book are either royalty-free images, used under license from their respective copyright holders, or images that are in the public domain.

© Copyright 2021 by NurseEdu.com - All rights reserved.

ISBN: 978-1-952914-13-3

FREE BONUS

FREE Download – Just Visit:

NurseEdu.com/bonus

TABLE OF CONTENTS

Chapter Start: NCLEX-RN
Mental Health: 100 Questions 1

CHAPTER START:

NCLEX-RN MENTAL HEALTH: 100 QUESTIONS

1. The nurse on the mental health unit is admitting a new patient for observation. The nurse knows that the DSM-5 states that causes and symptoms of mental illness can be influenced by which of the following?

   A. Culture and ethnic factors
   B. Birth order
   C. Sexual orientation
   D. Occupation and social status

Rationale:

Correct answer: A.

The DSM-5 is the Diagnostic and Statistical Manual of Mental Disorders, fifth edition, published by the American Psychiatric Association (APA). It is considered the universal authority for psychiatric diagnosis. According to the DSM-5, evidence exists that symptoms and causes of mental illness are influenced by cultural and ethnic factors.

B is incorrect because birth order does not influence mental illness, according to the DSM-5.

C is incorrect because the DSM-5 does not include sexual orientation as a significant influence on mental illness.

D is incorrect because occupation and social status may influence mental illness, but these are not listed as causes by the DSM-5.

2. The nurse on the inpatient psychiatric unit is preparing a patient for the termination phase of the nurse-patient relationship. Which nursing task is most appropriate for the nurse to implement?

   A. Planning short-term goals
   B. Making appropriate referrals
   C. Developing realistic solutions
   D. Identifying expected outcomes

Rationale:

Correct answer: B.

The nurse-patient relationship is divided into three phases: orientation (establishing rapport, developing a therapeutic environment), working (exploration of client's behavior, identification of coping skills), and termination. The termination phase of the nurse-patient relationship includes evaluating patient performance, evaluating achievement of outcomes, planning for future needs, making referrals, and dealing with common behaviors associated with termination.

A is incorrect because short-term goals are part of the working phase.

C is incorrect because developing realistic solutions is part of the working phase.

D is incorrect because identifying expected outcomes is part of the working phase.

3. The nurse in the emergency room is caring for a young adult male patient who has just been brought in by paramedics following a severe motor vehicle accident (MVA). Which mental health characteristic can help this patient to adapt after suffering tragedy and trauma?

   A. Dependence
   B. Resilience
   C. Pessimism
   D. Altruism

Rationale:

Correct answer: B.

A characteristic that helps people cope with loss and trauma is resilience. Resilience gives people psychological strength to cope in the midst of hardship, stress, trauma, change, and loss.

A is incorrect because dependence is relying on others for care and decision-making. The nurse should help the patient to stay as independent as possible after an MVA.

C is incorrect because pessimism is the belief that things will most likely go wrong rather than right.

D is incorrect because altruism is the act of putting others before oneself.

4. The nurse is working with a patient with Alzheimer's disease with frequent episodes of emotional lability. The patient frequently asks to talk to her husband, who the nurse knows died 17 years ago. Which of the following nursing interventions is most appropriate for this patient?

   A. Attempt to use humor to distract the patient from thinking about her husband.
   B. Talk with the patient and explore the reasoning for the patient's mood swings.
   C. Take the framed picture of the husband off the wall and ask the patient to talk about her husband.

D. Remind the patient that her husband died years ago and redirect the patient's attention.

Rationale:

Correct answer: C.

Alzheimer's disease is a form of dementia that interferes with memory, thinking, and behavior and is not a normal part of aging. Patients with Alzheimer's disease frequently have labile moods, ask repetitive questions, and often live in a reality from the past. When asking about a family member who is no longer alive, it is therapeutic to engage in conversation about that individual by looking at pictures and helping the patient to recall positive memories associated with the loved one. Often, talking about the deceased individual will help meet the patient's need to talk with him.

A is incorrect because, although distraction is used with Alzheimer's patients, they do not always have the cognitive ability to respond appropriately to humor.

B is incorrect because the patient with Alzheimer's does not have insight into her own behavior or awareness of causative factors.

D is incorrect because, although redirection is useful for Alzheimer's patients, it is not therapeutic to tell her that her husband is dead. The patient is living in a reality in which her husband is still alive. Telling her otherwise will confuse her.

5. The nurse on the inpatient psychiatric unit is leading a therapy group. The nurse is observing a paranoid patient who is suspicious and using projection. For which purpose is the projection used?

   A. To deny reality
   B. To deal with unacceptable feelings and thoughts
   C. To show resentment towards others
   D. To manipulate others

Rationale:

Correct answer: B.

Projection is attributing feelings, wishes, thoughts, or impulses that are perceived as inadequacies to others, in an attempt to reduce anxiety. Projection is common among patients with paranoid personality disorder. These patients often hold grudges, feel personally threatened by the actions of others, and may act hypersensitive, humorless, and serious.

A is incorrect because the patient displaying projection is not in denial of personal feelings. The *awareness* of self-perceived feelings, thoughts, and impulses increases personal anxiety. Thus, these feelings are projected onto others as an attempt to reduce anxiety.

C is incorrect because showing resentment is not the purpose of projection, but rather an outcome.

D is incorrect because manipulation of others is more commonly seen with bipolar disorder and borderline personality disorder.

6. The nurse in the mental health clinic is interviewing a new patient with severe anxiety. The nurse would be most helpful to this patient by using which intervention?

   A. Give specific instructions and speak in concise statements.
   B. Ask the patient to identify the cause of the anxiety.
   C. Explain, in detail, the care plan, and offer reassurance.
   D. Dim the lights, instruct the patient to breathe slowly, and leave the room so the patient can rest.

Rationale:

Correct answer: A.

The patient with severe anxiety will have a narrowed field of perception. They are unable to follow long explanations, so the nurse should use specific and concise instructions. Environmental stimulation should be minimized when anxiety is high.

B is incorrect because patients with severe anxiety are unable to identify the cause. It is beneficial to assist the patient in verbalizing what she is currently thinking and feeling. Reducing the anxiety is a greater priority than identifying the cause of the anxiety.

C is incorrect because, although offering reassurance is therapeutic, a patient with severe anxiety has difficulty with concentration and cannot focus on a detailed explanation.

D is incorrect because, although stimulation should be reduced, a patient with severe anxiety should not be left alone.

7. The nurse who works in the mental health clinic runs in to a neighbor in a local grocery store. When the neighbor asks the nurse, "How is Frank doing? He's my best friend and goes to your clinic weekly." What is the most appropriate response by the nurse?

   A. "The law prevents me from discussing patient situations with you."

   B. "If you want to know about Frank, you need to ask him yourself."

C. "Because you're a friend, I can only tell you he's improving. But I can't give any other details."

D. "What's Frank's last name, so I can determine which Frank you are asking about?"

Rationale:

Correct answer: A.

The nurse is required to maintain confidentiality regarding Frank and his care. This is basic to the therapeutic relationship and is the patient's right. The nurse should be direct, but polite.

B is incorrect because it is blunt and does not acknowledge why revealing patient information is disrespectful and uncaring.

C is incorrect because it violates patient confidentiality.

D is incorrect because the nurse should not give out any information about any patient to the nurse's neighbor.

8. The nurse in the mental health clinic cares for a patient who is extremely afraid of driving over bridges. The nurse plans to use desensitization to help the patient cope effectively and overcome his fear. Which of the following is the desired outcome of desensitization?

   A. The patient verbalizes fears regarding bridges.

B. The patient voluntarily attends group therapy and discusses the origin of his fear of bridges.

C. The patient studies a community map with the nurse and makes plans to avoid crossing bridges to reach commonly visited destinations.

D. The patient can watch a video of a car crossing a bridge without an increase in anxiety levels.

Rationale:

Correct answer: D.

Desensitization assists the patient in overcoming a fear by gradually exposing the patient to the object, activity, or location which provokes the fear. Intense reactions to the stimulus can be reduced by repeated exposure to the stimulus in a weaker and milder form. The nurse can begin by showing the patient pictures of bridges, and then show a video of a vehicle crossing a bridge, and eventually have the patient ride in a car that crosses a bridge. This is an example of how desensitization can be effective for this patient's fear.

A is incorrect because verbalizing fears is the beginning of the process and not the desired outcome of desensitization.

B is incorrect because voluntarily attending group therapy and discussing the reasoning behind the fear is not an outcome of desensitization.

C is incorrect because learning how to avoid bridges is not a component of desensitization.

9. The mental health nurse is caring for a 26-year-old female following a suicide attempt. Which of the following statements by the nurse is characteristic of patient advocacy?

   A. The nurse says to the doctor: "Dr. Heath, I see you placed an order for fluoxetine. The patient does not want to take fluoxetine due to previous adverse effects that were experienced."
   B. The nurse says to the doctor: "Dr. Heath, the patient states she has attempted suicide three times in the past."
   C. The nurse says to the patient: "Could you tell me more about what made you feel this way and what caused you to try to hurt yourself?"
   D. The nurse says to the patient: "Let me show you around and tell you about the rules of the unit."

Rationale:

Correct answer: A.

Patient advocacy requires the nurse to actively support the patient's wishes in planning care. Communicating the patient's needs and wishes to other members of the healthcare team is a component of patient advocacy. If the nurse is aware of the patient's previous negative experience with a medication, informing the healthcare provider about the patient's concerns is appropriate, and maintains patient autonomy and independence.

B is incorrect because this statement is simply giving information, not advocating for the patient in any way.

C is incorrect because although this is therapeutic communication, it is not an example of patient advocacy.

D is incorrect because giving the patient an orientation and explanation of rules and expectations is appropriate, but is not patient advocacy.

10. A patient jumps up angrily during a group activity in the inpatient psychiatric unit and throws his chair out the window. The staff has difficulty de-escalating the patient, so security is called and the patient is placed in restraints. Which of the following pieces of documentation indicates the safeguarding of this patient's rights?

    A. An order is signed by the healthcare provider for PRN soft wrist restraints.

B. The nurse documents: Informed consent for restraints not obtained.

C. The nurse documents: Circulation checked every 30 minutes while in wrist restraints.

D. The nurse documents: Before restraints were applied, staff attempted less restrictive measures unsuccessfully.

Rationale:

Correct answer: D.

All patients have the right to be free from restraints. If restraints are to be used, less restrictive measures should be tried first. This documentation indicates the patient was not placed in restraints until after less restrictive measures failed in de-escalating the patient's behavior.

A is incorrect because restraints cannot be ordered to be used PRN.

B is incorrect because informed consent *should* be obtained for the use of restraints. If the patient is belligerent, disoriented, or otherwise unable to give consent, then consent by proxy must be obtained.

C is incorrect because it is an example of good nursing care and safe practices, but does not address patient rights.

11. The new psychiatric nurse is teaching a newly admitted patient about the psychiatric unit. When teaching this patient, which of the following statements by the nurse is inappropriate?

   A. "Patients are expected to participate in activities and groups every day."
   B. "I will give you a group schedule that you should attend."
   C. "I lead a psychotherapy group that you will attend."
   D. "You will visit with the healthcare provider daily for one-on-one sessions."

Rationale:

Correct answer: C.

Psychotherapy is not performed by new psychiatric nurses, rather by a psychiatrist or psychologist. Psychotherapy is performed to help patients learn more about their mental health disorder as well as moods, thoughts, and behaviors to help them better respond to difficult situations and regain control of their life.

A is incorrect because expecting patient participation in group activities is appropriate. In psychiatric care settings, expectations must be clearly communicated upon admission so the patient knows what is expected of him.

B is incorrect because giving a patient a schedule of groups for attendance is appropriate. Patients are more likely to cooperate with the plan of care if they know what to expect throughout their day and where they are expected to be at different times.

D is incorrect because informing the patient of daily sessions with the healthcare provider is appropriate.

12. A patient is brought into the emergency room by a friend after "taking something" an hour ago. The patient is hallucinating, breathing rapidly, hyperactive, behaving in an agitated manner, and has a bloody nose. Which of the following substances does the nurse suspect the patient took?

    A. Heroin
    B. Cocaine
    C. LSD
    D. Marijuana

Rationale:

Correct answer: B.

Cocaine is a CNS stimulant and can make patients agitated, experience hallucinations, and dilate the pupils. Patients may lose contact with reality and experience intense happiness as well as experience tachycardia, hypertension, and hyperthermia. Cocaine is a powerful vasoconstrictor and can decrease myocardial oxygen supply. Nursing care for the patient who is intoxicated with cocaine includes: monitor the airway (may need intubation and suction), give IV fluids, monitor cardiac function, and keep the environment quiet.

A is incorrect because heroin is a narcotic. Heroin intoxication will lead to euphoria, impairment in judgment, respiratory depression, and papillary constriction.

C is incorrect because LSD intoxication will lead to grandiosity, hallucinations, synesthesia, and increased vital signs.

D is incorrect because marijuana intoxication will lead to slowed reaction time, conjunctival redness, impaired judgment, and social withdrawal. Hyperactivity would occur as a sign of withdrawal from a cannabis product and would not happen within one hour of using it.

13. The nurse is speaking with the family member of an older patient that was admitted yesterday. The family member tells the nurse she is hurt when the patient accuses her of stealing her belongings. Which of the following is the most therapeutic response by the nurse?

   A. "Don't take it personally; she doesn't mean it."

B. "Have you tried discussing this with her?"

C. "This must be difficult for you and your mother."

D. "Next time, ask her where she last saw her belongings."

Rationale:

Correct answer: C.

To demonstrate empathy towards the family member, the nurse should first show this by paraphrasing the feelings that have been verbalized to build rapport. Then, after gathering more information about the feelings and experiences, the nurse can give therapeutic suggestions for coping.

A is incorrect because verbalization of feelings should be encouraged ahead of giving advice.

B is incorrect because this response does not encourage verbalization of feelings and is a closed-ended question that doesn't elicit much information from the family member.

D is incorrect because verbalization of feelings should be encouraged ahead of telling the family member what to do.

14. The nurse is educating a patient regarding a new prescription for diazepam. Which of the following does the nurse include in the teaching?

    A. Avoid alcohol consumption.
    B. You can continue with your normal daily activities.
    C. Limit fluid intake.
    D. You can still drink coffee or tea.

Rationale:

Correct answer: A.

Valium is a benzodiazepine that causes central nervous system (CNS) depression. Consuming alcohol or other CNS depressants with it will potentiate effects and can cause hypotension, respiratory depression, and lethargy.

B is incorrect because the patient must be taught to avoid activities that require being alert due to the depressant effects of the medication. The patient should not drive or operate machinery after taking the medication. Other activities that require alertness, such as working or taking care of young children, may be difficult as well.

C is incorrect because adequate fluids should be encouraged when taking diazepam.

D is incorrect because stimulants, such as caffeine, can decrease the therapeutic effect of diazepam. The patient should be taught to avoid caffeine or other stimulants.

15. The nursing student is working with the psychiatric nurse on the mental health unit. The nursing student learns that which statement regarding mental illness is correct?

    A. Mental illness is a form of individual nonconformity to societal norms.
    B. Mental illness is suspected when an individual behaves irrationally and illogically.
    C. The mental illness definition and treatment approaches have changed over time and may be defined differently by various cultural groups.
    D. Mental illness is evaluated by examining an individual's control over behavior and their appraisal of reality.

Rationale:

Correct answer: C.

The definition of mental illness has changed over time with changes in systems and culture, time period, and with new and expanded definitions of mental health disorders.

A is incorrect because individual nonconformity is not considered mental illness. While it is true that many mentally ill patients do not conform to societal norms, the statement is not a fact.

B is incorrect because irrational and illogical behavior may be due to other medications or circumstances. These behaviors are not necessarily signs of mental illness.

D is incorrect because mental illness is evaluated by examining an individual's behavioral patterns and ability to function in day-to-day life.

16. A nursing student is working with the nurse on the mental health unit. The nurse is teaching the student about the positive impact nurses can make on legislation regarding mental illness treatment by:

    A. Becoming an advanced practice nurse, such as a Mental Health Nurse Practitioner.
    B. Advocating for treatment equality by a reduction in the stigma of mental illness.
    C. Advocating for laws supporting involuntary long-term commitment.
    D. Discouraging abuse of the system through inappropriate psychiatric admissions by advocating reduced insurance benefits for mental health.

Rationale:

Correct answer: B.

Nurses who make themselves aware of legislation and are active in mental health awareness promotion and equal mental health treatment can help achieve parity or equal treatment possibilities for the mentally ill.

A is incorrect because becoming politically active does not require an advanced practice degree. All Registered Nurses are capable of impacting legislation related to mental illness. Joining the legislative committee of a nursing professional association, such as the American Nurses Association, requires only an RN license.

C is incorrect because mentally ill patients are often the victims of laws that incarcerate or hospitalize them involuntarily without a full investigation into treatment options. These laws do not help advocate for equal care for the mentally ill.

D is incorrect because reduced insurance benefits for mental health will have a detrimental effect on individuals' ability to find affordable mental health care, and this is not a desirable outcome.

17. The nurse at the mental health community center is educating an elderly patient regarding a new prescription for lorazepam for generalized anxiety disorder. Which of the following does the nurse include when teaching this patient?

   A. Avoid foods rich in tyramine.

B. Notify your healthcare provider if you notice a change in your breathing.

C. You can stop taking the medication when you feel your anxiety is under control.

D. Take double the normal dosage if a dose is missed.

Rationale:

Correct answer: B.

Lorazepam, a benzodiazepine, is safer for use in the elderly than some other antianxiety medications. These medications can cause respiratory depression, so changes in respiratory function, such as decreased respiratory rate, should be reported immediately.

A is incorrect because patients taking monoamine oxidase inhibitors (MAOIs) should avoid foods rich in tyramine, as this can contribute to a hypertensive crisis. Tyramine does not need to be avoided with benzodiazepines.

C is incorrect because lorazepam can cause dependency, so abruptly stopping the medication should be avoided to prevent withdrawal and convulsions. The healthcare provider should be contacted before stopping the medication, so the patient can be given instructions for weaning.

D is incorrect because doubling a dose of lorazepam may intensify central nervous system depression, which is unsafe. If a dose is missed, the patient should take the next dose as scheduled.

18. The student nurse in the inpatient psychiatric unit is learning about anxiety. The student nurse learns that anxiety is caused by which of the following?

    A. An objective threat
    B. A subjectively perceived threat
    C. Hostility turned to self
    D. Masked depression

Rationale:

Correct answer: B.

Anxiety is caused by something the person perceives as a threat. Anxiety is characterized by tachycardia, fear, tachypnea, increased blood pressure, and feelings of loss of control.

A is incorrect because an objective threat typically causes fear. An objective threat is an actual threat that the patient can see, hear, or smell. Anxiety may result as well, but anxiety more commonly is related to a threat perceived to be real by the patient (but that threat is not always objectively real).

C is incorrect because internalized hostility is commonly seen with depression, not anxiety.

D is incorrect because masked depression causes mania.

19. The nurse on the inpatient psychiatric unit is observing a patient who has increasingly aggressive behavior. Which of the following approaches should be used last?

    A. Acknowledge the patient's behavior.
    B. Maintain a safe distance from the patient.
    C. Take the patient to a quiet area.
    D. Initiate measures to confine the patient.

Rationale:

Correct answer: D.

Confining an aggressive patient can escalate the behavior, so this is the least helpful approach. Confinement or seclusion should not be initiated by the nurse until all other measures have been attempted to de-escalate the patient.

A is incorrect because acknowledging behavior is appropriate during the escalation of aggression.

B is incorrect because maintaining a safe distance is appropriate during the escalation of aggression. The nurse should also encourage other patients to maintain a safe distance from the aggressive patient.

C is incorrect because decreased environmental stimulation (such as a non-crowded, quiet area with dimmed lights) is appropriate during the escalation of aggression.

20. Which of the following is the primary nursing intervention for a child who is a victim of domestic violence?

    A. Teach coping skills.
    B. Determine if other children in the home are also being abused.
    C. Assess for injury and ensure the safety of the child.
    D. Report the abuse to the proper authorities.

Rationale:

Correct answer: C.

The nurse's primary consideration for a child being abused is physical safety. Physical injuries should be assessed and cared for to ensure physiologic safety and integrity. This comes ahead of any other nursing interventions.

A is incorrect because teaching coping skills is not the primary nursing intervention and may not be appropriate for a child.

B is incorrect because the physical safety of the patient is a priority over assessing others.

D is incorrect because, although the nurse has a legal obligation to report the abuse, this is not a greater priority than the physical care of the child.

21. The nurse on the inpatient psychiatric unit is caring for a 72-year-old male patient who is experiencing alcohol withdrawal. The patient is hallucinating and confused. What is the priority intervention for this patient?

    A. Monitor vital signs hourly and stay with the patient.
    B. Provide a quiet, dim room, and check on the patient every hour.
    C. Encourage fluids.
    D. Administer chlordiazepoxide.

Rationale:

Correct answer: A.

Patients experiencing withdrawal typically have elevated pulse and blood pressure. The vital signs should be monitored hourly and the nurse should remain with the patient. Excessively elevated pulse and blood pressure can indicate the patient is experiencing delirium tremens.

B is incorrect because the patient should be in a quiet, well-lit, and secure environment. The nurse should not leave a hallucinating patient alone.

C is incorrect because the patient needs fluids and IM or IV vitamin B supplements, but the patient is also at risk for vomiting and aspiration, so fluids should be monitored carefully.

D is incorrect because chlordiazepoxide should not be used on the elderly due to its long half-life and risk for toxicity.

22. The psychiatric nurse is caring for a 24-year-old patient admitted for a manic state of bipolar disorder. The nurse knows that, according to Maslow's needs theory, which symptom is a priority for care?

    A. Rapid speech
    B. Thoughts of grandiosity
    C. Lack of sleep
    D. Hyperactive behavior

Rationale:

Correct answer: C.

Maslow's Hierarchy of Needs theory demonstrates that basic needs including food, water, air, and sleep are the priority. The nurse is most concerned with the patient's physical health and safety. Manic patients can go up to several days without sleep, depriving their bodies of the rest needed to physically function. The nurse should encourage the manic patient to take short naps, when possible.

A is incorrect because rapid speech is a symptom of mania, but does not pose a significant threat to the patient's physical health.

B is incorrect because thoughts of grandiosity are a symptom of mania, but do not pose a health threat unless the patient specifically is engaging in dangerous behavior.

D is incorrect because hyperactive behavior is commonly seen with mania but not as much of a physical threat as lack of sleep.

23. The nursing student is learning about the basics of mental health nursing. When a patient states, "Nobody could ever love me, so I will always be alone," the student knows this is an example of which of the following?

    A. Emotional consequence
    B. Aversion
    C. Self-Actualization
    D. Schema

Rationale:

Correct answer: D.

According to Beck's theory, schemas are assumptions uniquely created about oneself. The example in this patient's statement is a negative schema.

A is incorrect because the emotional consequence is the result of a negative thinking process.

B is incorrect because aversion is a type of psychological therapy in which the patient is exposed to a stimulus while concurrently being subjected to a form of discomfort; the goal is to cause the patient to associate the stimulus with unpleasant sensations, to suppress the behavior.

C is incorrect because self-actualization is found at the top of Maslow's Hierarchy of Needs.

24. The new nurse on the inpatient psychiatric unit is learning about patient advocacy. The nurse learns that patient advocacy is characterized by which of the following actions?

    A. Encouraging the patient to express feelings regarding an experience.
    B. Assessing the patient for injuries.
    C. Postponing a physical assessment until the patient is calm.
    D. Explaining to the patient that the reactions are normal.

Rationale:

Correct answer: C.

Attempting physical assessment when a patient is agitated or aggressive can result in injury to the patient and nurse. Postponing the physical assessment until the patient is calm can protect the patient from physical harm and is thus patient advocacy.

A is incorrect because this is an example of a nurse as a counselor.

B is incorrect because this is an example of a nurse as a technician.

D is incorrect because this is an example of a nurse as a teacher.

25. The psychiatric unit nurse tells the nursing student she only believes in the biological model of mental illness. The student knows which of the following is true of the biological model?

    A. Culture, environment, social, and spiritual influences do not impact mental health.
    B. It does not explain every symptom characteristic of mental illness.
    C. It is the oldest and most reliable model for mental illness explanation.

D. It is most popular among psychiatrists.

Rationale:

Correct answer: A.

Cultural, environmental, social, and spiritual influences are not seen as influences on mental health, according to the biological model. This model is also known as the neurophysiological model, in which the belief is that humans consist of natural functions designed by nature. Mental illness is the result of malfunctioning neurophysiological processes.

B is incorrect because the biological model can explain every symptom of mental illness.

C is incorrect because the biological model is not the oldest and most reliable model of explaining mental illness. The first and oldest model ever used to explain mental illness was the spiritual model.

D is incorrect because the biological model is not the most popular among psychiatrists.

26. The female 22-year-old patient in the community mental health center tells the nurse she hasn't slept at all for the past week. Which of the following responses by the nurse is most appropriate?

    A. "I understand, you must be tired."

B. "Really?"

C. "You're experiencing difficulty sleeping?"

D. "I have difficulty sleeping sometimes, too."

Rationale:

Correct answer: C.

This response uses the therapeutic communication technique of restatement. It repeats the patient's theme and uses a tone that may elicit more information from the patient. This type of communication demonstrates that the nurse has heard what has been said and allows the nurse to get a more specific perception of the problem.

A is incorrect because, while it is a reassuring response, it does not encourage the patient to talk about the problem.

B is incorrect because this statement does not encourage the patient to talk about the problem.

D is incorrect because this statement moves the focus away from the patient and focuses on the nurse, instead. I-statements are not *always* non-therapeutic, but students should learn to look for responses that maintain the focus on the patient.

27. The nurse is caring for a patient admitted for alcohol detoxification. The nurse notes the patient is exhibiting muscle twitching, irritability, a blood pressure of 168/88,

and a temperature of 101.2°F (38.4°C). Which of the following nursing actions is best?

A. Monitor for delirium tremens.
B. Monitor for Korsakoff's syndrome.
C. Evaluate for potential esophageal varices.
D. Monitor for Wernicke's syndrome.

Rationale:

Correct answer: A.

Delirium tremens (DTs, also known as alcohol withdrawal delirium) are due to extreme nervous system irritability as a result of sudden cessation of alcohol intake. The nurse should be alert for anxiety, uncontrollable fear, tremors, agitation, and incontinence. The goals of management are to give adequate sedation to allow the patent to rest and recover without a peripheral vascular collapse. The room should remain lighted to prevent visual hallucinations. Sedation reduces agitation and promotes sleep.

B is incorrect because Korsakoff's syndrome is a chronic nervous system disorder associated with long-term alcohol abuse and thiamine deficiency. Symptoms include the memory loss of recent events. This is not the nurse's greatest concern during acute alcohol withdrawal.

C is incorrect because esophageal varices (dilated blood vessels in the esophagus) are a complication of liver cirrhosis. Varices are commonly seen in alcoholic patients, but not specifically when in withdrawal. Symptoms include hematemesis and hypotension, and other signs of hypovolemic shock.

D is incorrect because Wernicke's syndrome is a chronic nervous system disorder characterized by irregular eye movements, diplopia, and a lack of coordination and confusion, as a result of chronic alcoholism. DT is the greater concern in acute withdrawal from alcohol.

28. The nurse is caring for a patient admitted with major depression. When discussing medications that affect neurotransmitters, the patient asks, "What are those?" What is the best response by the nurse?

    A. "Neurotransmitters are very complicated to explain, just know the medication will benefit your mood."
    B. "Neurotransmitters are the chemical messengers of the brain that regulate specific functions."
    C. "Neurotransmitters, or lack of neurotransmitters, can be the cause of your depression."
    D. "I can have the healthcare provider explain neurotransmitters to you."

Rationale:

Correct answer: B.

Neurotransmitters are chemicals released by neurons in the brain. These chemicals are messengers that can influence the functions of the brain. They have been shown to affect mood when their production or lack thereof is altered, leading to mood abnormalities including depression. Many antidepressant medications target specific neurotransmitters, such as serotonin or dopamine. The nurse should answer the patient's question and provide factual information. This will help educate the patient, increase a trusting relationship, and encourage the patient to ask more questions for clarification.

A is incorrect because this response does not answer the patient's question and it gives false reassurance. The nurse should be able to communicate therapeutically and give information that the patient can understand.

C is incorrect because it is a simplistic response and does not answer the patient's question adequately. An important component of therapeutic communication is to address patients' concerns and answer questions with factual information.

D is incorrect because this response passes the buck to the healthcare provider. Patient education is a primary nursing responsibility, and nurses are expected to have knowledge of human anatomy, disease processes, and medications. When possible, the nurse should address the patient's concerns within the nurse's knowledge, and only choose to call the healthcare provider after personally having the discussion with the patient.

29. The home health nurse is working with a patient who has moderate stage dementia. The priority nursing intervention the nurse should implement is ensuring which of the following?

    A. The patient receives adequate nutrition and hydration.
    B. The patient will reminisce to decrease isolation.
    C. The patient remains in a safe environment.
    D. The patient independently performs safe care.

Rationale:

Correct answer: C.

Dementia is a decline in intellectual function. Symptoms include memory loss, impaired language (forgetting the name of common objects), the loss of the ability to think abstractly, and ultimately, the loss of the ability to perform self-care activities, leading to a loss of social independence. The patient with moderate-stage dementia is at an elevated risk for injury as cognitive ability deteriorates affecting balance, strength, and coordination. Thus, a safe environment is the primary nursing concern.

A is incorrect because adequate nutrition and hydration are important, but not a greater priority than patient safety.

B is incorrect because reminiscing is helpful for meeting the patient's psychosocial needs, but physical needs take priority.

D is incorrect because independent safe care may be unattainable in patients with moderate-stage dementia.

30. The nurse in the mental health clinic is evaluating a patient for potential early-stage dementia. Which of the following would the nurse expect to see to help confirm this diagnosis?

    A. Slurred speech
    B. Insidious onset
    C. Clouding of consciousness
    D. Decreased ability to swallow

Rationale:

Correct answer: B.

Dementia is characterized by gradual (insidious) onset and then progressive deterioration. Dementia initially causes disturbances in memory of recent conversations, names, or events. Apathy and depression are also seen early. As dementia progresses, impaired communication, disorientation, poor judgment, and behavior changes may be seen. Late-stage dementia may impair swallowing, speaking, and ambulating.

A is incorrect because slurred speech is a characteristic of delirium, not early dementia. Late-stage dementia patients may have difficulty talking.

C is incorrect because the clouding of consciousness is a characteristic of delirium.

D is incorrect because decreased ability to swallow is a later sign of dementia.

31. A patient in the community health clinic is in for a follow-up after a new prescription of haloperidol. The patient is displaying pill-rolling tremors and muscle rigidity. The nurse should speak to the healthcare provider about which of the following concerns?

   A. Tardive dyskinesia
   B. Pseudo-parkinsonism
   C. Akinesia
   D. Dystonia

Rationale:

Correct answer: B.

Pseudo-parkinsonism is a side effect of some antipsychotic drugs, such as haloperidol. It is characterized by mask-like facial expressions, pill-rolling tremors, and muscle rigidity.

A is incorrect because tardive dyskinesia is a result of long-term antipsychotic medication use, such as risperidone. The extrapyramidal characteristics include involuntary movements of mouth and tongue, such as chewing motions, sucking, tongue thrusting, and lip-smacking. Other involuntary movements of the extremities or the trunk may be seen.

C is incorrect because akinesia is loss of voluntary muscle movement, including feelings of weakness and muscle fatigue. Akinesia is characteristic of patients diagnosed with Parkinson's.

D is incorrect because dystonia a state of abnormal muscle tone resulting in muscular spasm and abnormal posture, typically due to neurological disease or a side effect of drug therapy. This patient is not exhibiting dystonia.

32. The nurse in the inpatient psychiatric unit is caring for a 15-year-old recently diagnosed with borderline personality disorder. Which of the following behaviors supports this diagnosis?

A. Lack of self-esteem, impulsive behavior, and strong dependency.
B. Social withdrawal, inadequacy, and sensitivity to rejection and criticism
C. Suspicion, hypervigilance, and coldness
D. Preoccupation with perfection, order, and a need for control

Rationale:

Correct answer: A.

Borderline personality disorder is characterized by a lack of self-esteem, impulsive behavior, and strong dependency. Many borderline personality disorder patients are women who have experienced sexual abuse. These patients often seek brief and intense relationships and have a tendency to be manipulative and blame others for their personal problems. Self-mutilation is common. Nursing interventions for borderline patients include encouragement of expression of the person's feelings, limit-setting, group therapy, empathy, and the use of behavioral contracts to reduce self-harm.

B is incorrect because it describes avoidant personality.

C is incorrect because it describes paranoid personality.

D is incorrect because it describes obsessive-compulsive disorder.

33. The nurse has administered scheduled medications to four patients in the psychiatric unit. The nurse knows that which of the following patients should be closely monitored for fluid and electrolyte imbalance?

   A. 56-year-old female taking lithium
   B. 44-year-old male taking clozapine
   C. 27-year-old female taking diazepam
   D. 38-year-old male taking amitriptyline

Rationale:

Correct answer: A.

Lithium is used as a mood stabilizer in patients diagnosed with bipolar disorder. It is a positively charged ion which can affect neuronal electrical conductivity. Lithium can cause sodium loss that can affect the heart or induce convulsions. Lithium also causes extreme diuresis and can lead to dehydration. Patients taking lithium must be encouraged to meet their fluid needs by taking up to 3 L of fluid PO daily and increase salt in the diet.

B is incorrect because clozapine blocks dopamine receptors and does not have an effect on fluid or electrolyte balances. Clozapine can cause EKG changes, specifically a long QT complex.

C is incorrect because diazepam is a benzodiazepine that inhibits brain electrical activity and has no effect on fluid or electrolyte balances. Diazepam can cause lethargy, hypotension, and respiratory depression.

D is incorrect because amitriptyline is a tricyclic antidepressant that blocks the reuptake of norepinephrine and has no effect on fluid or electrolyte balances. It can cause sedation, confusion, and anticholinergic side-effects (dry mouth, blurred vision).

34. The nurse in the inpatient psychiatric unit is performing an interview with a patient who is displaying an escalation of angry behavior. The nurse demonstrates awareness of patient rights by which of the following actions?

    A. Taking a directive role in verbalizing feelings
    B. Using an authoritarian, confrontational approach
    C. Placing the patient in seclusion
    D. Applying restraints

Rationale:

Correct answer: A.

Taking a directive role in encouraging the verbalization of patient feelings can help with de-escalating anger and aggression. The nurse should speak in one-thought sentences, be consistent, and state the patient's name from time to time.

B is incorrect because an authoritarian, confrontational approach can be threatening and add to patient tension.

C is incorrect because isolation is not utilized until less restrictive measures are attempted.

D is incorrect because restraints are not applied until less restrictive measures are attempted. If restraints are needed, the least restrictive device should be used to prevent the patient from injuring themselves and others.

35. A patient in the inpatient psychiatric unit believes his food is being poisoned. Which of the following techniques should the nurse use to encourage this patient to eat?

    A. Sit and eat with the patient, and use therapeutic silence.
    B. Share personal food choice preferences.
    C. Document reasons why the patient is avoiding eating.
    D. Offer information about the need for proper nutrition.

Rationale:

Correct answer: A.

Sitting and eating with the patient can help dispel the patient's paranoia. Therapeutic silence can be used to give the patient time to eat, reinforce the trusting relationship, and establish rapport. Then the patient can be encouraged to discuss their concerns and feelings.

B is incorrect because sharing personal food choice preferences is not patient-centered. This action focuses on the nurse and will not encourage the patient to eat.

C is incorrect because documentation is appropriate but does not encourage the patient to eat.

D is incorrect because the patient's problem is not a lack of knowledge about nutrition. This patient is experiencing paranoia.

36. A patient is in the community health center describing recent emotional changes to the nurse. The patient explains, "I have lost interest in gardening and running, I feel sad but I don't know why, and I just want to sleep all the time." Which of the following mental health diagnoses does the nurse suspect?

   A. Bipolar disorder
   B. Dissociative identity disorder
   C. Depressive disorder
   D. Schizophrenia

Rationale:

Correct answer: C.

Depression is characterized by a loss of interest, feelings of sadness, loss of energy, and sleeping more often or difficulty sleeping. This patient has described symptoms of depression with the loss of interest in hobbies and favorite activities, feelings of sadness with no explanation, and a desire to sleep more.

A is incorrect because bipolar disorder is characterized by feelings of extreme sadness and lethargy, alternating with elevated mood and energy. Bipolar patients often have a flight of ideas, lack inhibitions, and are easily distractible.

B is incorrect because dissociative identity disorder is characterized by the loss of the track of time or memory impairment and two or more personalities.

D is incorrect because schizophrenia is characterized by losing touch with reality and abnormal social behavior. These patients are often withdrawn with a flat affect, are socially inept, and suffer from hypochondriasis or suspiciousness.

37. There is one bed available in the locked psychiatric unit. The nursing supervisor knows which of the following patients would be most appropriate for involuntary admission to this last remaining bed?

   A. A 21-year-old female college student displaying anxiety who has missed college classes and work.

B. A 33-year-old male attorney with depression.

C. A 28-year-old female elementary school teacher who does not seem to be in touch with reality found walking in the middle of traffic.

D. A 56-year-old librarian experiencing memory loss and occasional confusion.

Rationale:

Correct answer: C.

Patients who are unable to protect themselves or who are at risk for self-harm are the most appropriate candidates for inpatient involuntary psychiatric admission.

A is incorrect because anxiety and withdrawal from activities and commitments do not meet the criteria for involuntary admission to the psychiatric facility.

B is incorrect because depression does not meet the criteria for involuntary admission. The depressed patient must be displaying behavior that suggests a risk for danger to self or others, to be considered for voluntary admission.

D is incorrect because memory loss and confusion do not meet the criteria for involuntary admission.

38. The nurse manager of a new inpatient psychiatric unit is reviewing the structural plans for the construction of the

facility. The nurse manager knows the most important safety precaution for preventing the most common type of suicides attempted by inpatients is:

A. Breakaway closet bars for hanging prevention.
B. Locked windows in patient rooms and dining areas.
C. Double-locked doors.
D. Platform beds for prevention of crush injuries.

Rationale:

Correct answer: A.

The most common type of inpatient suicide is hanging. Breakaway closet bars are essential in an inpatient psychiatric unit to prevent this from occurring. Other measures that can be taken to reduce inpatient hangings include stainless-steel boxes around plumbing fixtures and 1:1 supervision.

B is incorrect because locked windows are important safety measures but do not address the most common form of inpatient suicide: hangings.

C is incorrect because double-locked doors are important safety measures to prevent escaping but do not address hangings.

D is incorrect because platform beds are important safety measures but do not address hangings.

39. The nurse in the inpatient psychiatric unit is having a one-on-one session with a patient. The patient tells the nurse, "The FBI is out to get me." What is the best response by the nurse?

    A. "The FBI is not out to get you."
    B. "I do not believe that."
    C. "I don't know anything about that, but I do understand that you are afraid of being harmed."
    D. "What makes you think that?"

Rationale:

Correct answer: C.

This statement by the nurse presents the patient with reality and also acknowledges how the patient feels. It is important for the nurse to share factual information with the patient about reality but also not to dismiss the patient's concerns.

A is incorrect because the response is dismissive and disagrees with the patient's false belief which could make the patient feel challenged.

B is incorrect because the response disagrees with the patient's false belief and does not express an understanding of the patient's fear. This response may make the patient feel challenged which does not benefit the nurse-patient relationship.

D is incorrect because it encourages the patient to unnecessarily explore the false statement.

40. The nursing supervisor is reviewing patient charts on the inpatient unit for potential discharges. Which of the following patients would benefit most from a partial-hospitalization program?

    A. A patient who is suicidal and states he has a plan.
    B. A patient who abused substances and is being discharged after alcohol rehabilitation.
    C. A patient with schizophrenia, who has stopped taking antipsychotics and is decompensated.
    D. A patient with mild depression starting outpatient therapy.

Rationale:

Correct answer: B.

A partial-hospitalization program is a step-down program for patients who need intensive short-term daily care and can return home every evening. This type of therapy would benefit the patient who has completed rehabilitation from alcohol abuse and needs help with relapse prevention.

A is incorrect because the patient who is suicidal (and admits he has a plan) needs inpatient hospitalization for safety.

C is incorrect because decompensation involves ineffective coping mechanisms in response to stress, resulting in personality disturbance or disintegration. This patient who is decompensated requires inpatient hospitalization for safety.

D is incorrect because the patient with mild depression does not need intensive therapy and can be managed on an outpatient basis.

41. A male patient admitted in the inpatient psychiatric unit for psychotic behavior spends most of the day at the locked exit shouting, "Let me out! There's nothing wrong with me! I don't belong here!" Which defense mechanism is being used by the patient?

    A. Denial
    B. Projection
    C. Regression
    D. Rationalization

    Rationale:

    Correct answer: A.

Denial is a defense mechanism used by patients to avoid reality and treat it as if it does not exist. This patient is using denial by saying he does not belong in the unit and has nothing wrong with him.

B is incorrect because projection is rejecting unacceptable feelings and attributing them to others.

C is incorrect because regression is returning to an earlier, less mature, more pleasant way of behavior.

D is incorrect because rationalization is justifying illogical or unreasonable actions, ideas, and feelings with acceptable explanations to satisfy both the patient and the listener.

42. The nurse in the mental health community center has worked with patients for many years. The nurse has seen many changes in mental illness and treatment over the years but knows the number one goal of treatment for mental illness is recovery. Recovery is described as:

    A. The ability to live, work, and participate in community events.
    B. No longer requiring mental health treatment.
    C. Better coping with symptoms.
    D. The journey over the patient's entire life.

Rationale:

Correct answer: A.

Recovery from mental illness is the result of a change in the individual's attitudes, roles, and behaviors which allows that person to have the ability to live, work, and participate in community events.

B is incorrect because many patients are in the recovery phase of mental illness, but they still require ongoing therapy or medical management of care. Recovery involves living a meaningful life, even with the limitations caused by the illness.

C is incorrect because better coping with symptoms is a good outcome, but not characteristic of recovery.

D is incorrect because recovery does not cover a patient's entire life.

43. A 15-year-old in the inpatient psychiatric unit was recently diagnosed with schizophrenia. When teaching the family regarding schizophrenia which of the following is most important?

    A. Symptoms of schizophrenia are due to imbalances in the brain.
    B. Genetic history is important for schizophrenia development.
    C. Schizophrenia is serious and affects every aspect of a person's functioning.

D. Distressing symptoms of schizophrenia can be relieved with medications.

Rationale:

Correct answer: D.

It is true that schizophrenia symptoms can be relieved with medications, and this provides an element of hope for the family.

A is incorrect because although this is truthful information, it does not provide any encouragement.

B is incorrect because there is a genetic component, but this is not important to provide to the family with a recent diagnosis.

C is incorrect because schizophrenia *does* affect every aspect of functioning, but this is not important to provide to the family with a recent diagnosis. This information focuses on the negative aspects of the diagnosis. The nurse should provide truthful information to the family and yet be encouraging as well.

44. A 43-year-old female patient with depression is being prepped for her first electroconvulsive therapy (ECT) treatment. Which of the following nursing actions is appropriate for the patient?

A. Teach the patient to report any confusion after the ECT, as this is a sign of a serious adverse reaction.
B. Position the patient supine, with arms at her side for the ECT.
C. Teach the patient that she should not expect to begin to see improvement in depression symptoms until after the third or fourth round of ECT.
D. Position the patient on their right side with the head of the bed elevated 30 degrees in case the patient vomits during the ECT.

Rationale:

Correct answer: B.

This is the correct position during ECT therapy.

A is incorrect because confusion is common after ECT treatment. The nurse should stay with the patent during the period of confusion.

C is incorrect because depression symptoms generally do not improve until 6-12 ECT treatments have been administered.

D is incorrect because the patient should be supine for an ECT.

45. The nurse is working with a 5-year-old child recently diagnosed with autistic disorder. Which of the following characteristics does the nurse expect to observe?

   A. Argumentativeness and disobedience
   B. Intolerance to change and disturbed relatedness
   C. Distractibility and impulsiveness
   D. Aggression and lying

Rationale:

Correct answer: B.

Autism is characterized by impaired social interaction, intolerance to change, communication challenges, and disturbed relatedness to others.

A is incorrect because argumentativeness and disobedience are characteristic of oppositional defiant disorder.

C is incorrect because distractibility and impulsiveness are characteristic of attention deficit disorder.

D is incorrect because aggression and lying are characteristic of conduct disorder.

46. Which of the following interventions should be avoided when caring for a child with autism?

A. Providing diversionary activities when the child acts out
B. Providing an atmosphere of acceptance
C. Providing safety measures
D. Rearranging the environment to keep the child interested

Rationale:

Correct answer: D.

Children with autism are resistant to change and do not adapt well. The nurse should maintain a consistent environment in order to be therapeutic.

A is incorrect because the child can be re-channeled through safe activities when acting out.

B is incorrect because acceptance will enhance a trusting relationship.

C is incorrect because providing safety measures prevents self-destructive behaviors such as hair pulling and head-banging.

47. Which of the following comments by the parent of a 3-year-old child could indicate potential child abuse?

   A. "Once my child is toilet-trained, they may still have accidents."

B. "When I tell my child to do something, I shouldn't have to tell him again."
C. "I expect my child to try to do some things unassisted, such as dressing and feeding himself."
D. "My 3-year-old loves the word *no*."

Rationale:

Correct answer: B.

Unrealistic expectations of a child are characteristic of abusive parents. Unrealistic expectations can lead to abuse when the expectations are not met.

A is incorrect because this is a realistic expectation for a 3-year-old child.

C is incorrect because it is a realistic expectation. Children should be encouraged to perform some activities independently as they are learning and growing.

D is incorrect because this is normal for a 3-year-old child and does not indicate abuse.

48. The nurse is caring for an agitated patient in the inpatient psychiatric unit. The nurse speaks with the patient privately to explore ways to help her calm down and avoid the need for restraints or seclusion. The nurse's actions are based on which of the following?

    A. Writ of habeas corpus
    B. Veracity

C. Least restrictive alternative doctrine
D. Bioethics

Rationale:

Correct answer: C.

The least restrictive alternative doctrine is using the most lenient means of achieving specific goals. These actions can prevent restraints or seclusion which can further agitate a patient and do not move a patient toward recovery and discharge.

A is incorrect because the writ of habeas corpus means to free the person and is a legal term.

B is incorrect because veracity is an ethical principle or guideline of accuracy and truthfulness.

D is incorrect because bioethics are ethics in healthcare.

49. A patient who survived a traumatic car accident in which her friend died four months ago, tells the nurse in the community mental health center that she can't concentrate, does not have an appetite, is unable to sleep, and feels guilty. The nurse knows this patient is experiencing which of the following?

   A. Adjustment disorder
   B. Somatoform disorder

C. Generalized anxiety disorder

D. Post-traumatic stress disorder

Rationale:

Correct answer: D.

Post-traumatic stress disorder (PTSD) is experienced immediately or delayed after a traumatic event. PTSD, which lasts for more than a month in time, is characterized by flashbacks of the event which cause stress, difficulty sleeping, irritability, and a lack of concentration.

A is incorrect because adjustment disorder is a maladaptive reaction to stressful events with anxiety, depression, and social impairment 3 months after a stressful event.

B is incorrect because somatoform disorder is anxiety with physical symptoms with or without an actual stressful event.

C is incorrect because generalized anxiety disorder is chronic excessive anxiety over small events and lasts more than 6 months.

50. The nurse manager is making rounds on patients in the mental health unit. Which patient is most appropriate for

release from the unit under the guidelines of Against Medical Advice (AMA)?

A. A 40-year-old male patient who has been in the unit for one week for depression; the healthcare provider encouraged him to stay one more day, but the patient refuses to stay.
B. An 80-year-old patient that was admitted with dementia and is demanding to go home.
C. A 24-year-old patient who is suicidal and wants to do outpatient counseling.
D. A 40-year-old patient who wants to remain admitted in the mental health unit, but whose spouse demands discharge.

Rationale:

Correct answer: A.

A discharge under AMA is used when the healthcare provider and patient do not agree. The patient cannot be a danger to themselves or others to be allowed to leave AMA. The patient must also be coherent and able to understand the healthcare provider's medical advice. This patient admitted for depression is not in danger of self-harm or harming others and is appropriate for AMA discharge.

B is incorrect because the patient with dementia is at risk of self-harm and is not able to cognitively understand the meaning of the medical advice.

C is incorrect because the actively suicidal patient is not appropriate for outpatient counseling or AMA discharge.

D is incorrect because a family member's opinion does not have an effect on AMA discharge.

51. A nurse performing a home visit for a female patient assesses multiple injuries at various stages of healing. The nurse is concerned about domestic abuse. Which of the following represents the best way for the nurse to communicate with this patient?

    A. "Is anyone threatening or hurting you?"
    B. "How long have you been being abused?"
    C. "Is there something bothering you?"
    D. "Many patients have felt safe confiding in me when they've been hurt by someone."

Rationale:

Correct answer: A.

The home care nurse must be skilled in interviewing techniques that are likely to elicit accurate information. Questions about potential abuse should be asked in private, away from others. This question validates the nurse's observation because it is a simple and direct question.

B is incorrect because it makes the assumption that the patient is being abused. This can be harmful to the nurse-patient relationship. Asking the patient directly if she is being hurt or threatened is the best (and first) way to directly address the potential abuse.

C is incorrect because it is an indirect question and is too vague.

D is incorrect because this statement focuses on other patients.

52. A 40-year-old woman with depression tells the nurse she is experiencing difficulty with sexual arousal and fears her husband will have an affair. Which of the following assessments will give the nurse the *least* significant information related to the patient's sexual difficulty?

    A. Assessment of over-the-counter and prescription medications used
    B. Assessment of current physical health status
    C. Assessment of education level attained and work experience
    D. Assessment of the quality of marriage and satisfaction with relationships at home

Rationale:

Correct answer: C.

The nurse should identify education level and work as having the least impact on this patient's sexual difficulty.

A is incorrect because numerous medications (MAOIs, SSRIs,) can affect sex drive and the ability to become aroused.

B is incorrect because physical health status can have a great influence on sexual arousal.

D is incorrect because the quality of marriage and satisfaction with interpersonal relationships can impact sexual health and arousal.

53. A patient in the mental health unit has paranoid schizophrenia, refuses to take his medications, and is running up and down the halls, banging his head with his fists. He is yelling, "Get the aliens out of my head!" On what basis can the nurse medicate this patient against his will?

    A. If the patient has taken the specific medication before and has not experienced adverse effects.
    B. If the patient poses a risk to harm himself or others.
    C. If the patient can make an informed decision about the medication.

D. If the patient is educated about the medication before the administration.

Rationale:

Correct answer: B.

The patient who poses a risk to themselves or others may be medicated against their will. No court hearing is necessary in an emergency for medication administration or treatment against a patient's will. Furthermore, in the case that the patient is *not* a direct threat to himself or others, if two physicians decide that a patient is incapable of giving informed consent to the medication, and the patient is in need of psychiatric medication, and will rapidly deteriorate without the medication, it can be administered against the patient's will.

A is incorrect because a lack of adverse effects with previous doses is not a legally valid reason to medicate against a patient's will.

C is incorrect because if the patient is capable of making an informed decision regarding medication, this is not enough information to justify medicating him against his will.

D is incorrect because a patient's education about the medication is not sufficient to medicate the patient against his will.

54. The student nurse is learning about age-appropriate stages of development in the inpatient psychiatric unit. Which would be the primary concern for a 22-year-old patient?

   A. Having an educational plan
   B. Feeling confident in personal identity
   C. Demonstrating an inability to trust others
   D. Difficulty identifying personal goals and vocational commitment

Rationale:

Correct answer: D.

According to Erikson's stages of development, the positive outcome for a young adult is to have a defined sense of self with plans for a vocational career and an interest in intimacy. The 22-year-old with difficulty identifying goals and plans for a vocation is at risk for not meeting the developmental tasks for the age group.

A is incorrect because plans for education and vocation are appropriate for a young adult, so this is not concerning to the nurse.

B is incorrect because feeling confident in personal identity suggests that the individual has met the developmental task for the adolescent stage.

C is incorrect because, although this is a negative outcome, trust is associated with the infancy stage, not the young adulthood stage.

55. The nurse is interviewing a new patient in the mental health community center. What is the nurse attempting to identify when asking the patient who is in the family and where they live?

    A. Boundaries
    B. Ethnicity
    C. Relationships
    D. Culture

Rationale:

Correct answer: A.

Family boundaries define who is inside and who is outside of the patient's system. The nurse should ask the patient who they consider to be family members and inquire about the home living situation.

B is incorrect because the question would not elicit information regarding ethnicity.

C is incorrect because the question would not address the nature of family relationships.

D is incorrect because the question would not elicit information regarding culture.

56. A patient in the inpatient psychiatric unit is displaying hostility toward one staff member in particular, for no known reason. The nurse knows this patient is displaying which of the following?

    A. Splitting
    B. Transference
    C. Countertransference
    D. Resistance

Rationale:

Correct answer: B.

In transference, the patient's past feelings, conflicts, and attitudes are transferred into present relationships, situations, and circumstances. Often negative feelings associated with a significant person in the patient's history are unconsciously assigned to another person, such as a member of the healthcare team.

A is incorrect because splitting, also known as all-or-nothing thinking, or black-and-white thinking is a defense mechanism commonly used by persons with personality disorder. When a patient demonstrates splitting, he is unable to see positive and negative aspects of self or others cohesively. Instead, he thinks in extremes, and people, self, and situations are perceived as *all* good, or *all* bad.

C is incorrect because countertransference is the opposite of transference: the nurse shifts feelings from his or her own personal past to the patient.

D is incorrect because resistance is the refusal of the patient to submit himself to care by the nurse.

57. The student nurse in the community mental health center is learning about mental health. Mental health is defined as which of the following?

   A. The ability to distinguish between what is real and what is not.
   B. A state of well-being in which one can realize his/her own abilities, cope with normal stresses of life, and work productively.
   C. The prevention of mental disorders and nursing care of patients during illness and rehabilitation.
   D. An absence of mental disorders and mental illness.

Rationale:

Correct answer: B.

Mental health is defined as a state of emotional as well as psychosocial well-being. A person who is mentally healthy is self-aware, self-directive, can solve problems, and can cope with a crisis without assistance.

A is incorrect because the ability to differentiate between reality and what is not real is ego function reality testing.

C is incorrect because it is the definition of mental health and psychiatric nursing.

D is incorrect because the mere absence of mental disorders and mental illness does not define mental health.

58. Which of the following methods would be optimal for the nurse to utilize when determining a patient's risk for suicide?

    A. Communicate non-judgmentally and offer the patient a pamphlet about help options available for those considering suicide.
    B. Observe the patient's behavior for cues of suicidal ideation.
    C. Ask the patient directly about any suicidal thoughts.
    D. Ask the patient about future plans.

Rationale:

Correct answer: C.

Direct questioning is best when it comes to determining a patient's risk for suicide. The nurse should use one-thought sentences and directly ask about thoughts of self-harm, using yes/no questions.

Note: A patient may initiate a discussion about suicidal ideation because of guilt, not wanting to be discovered, or lack of trust in the nurse.

Note: Generally, open-ended questions are better for helping the nurse to elicit information from patients regarding health status, lifestyle, and other situations. However, when the topic is suicide, asking a to-the-point yes/no question such as "Are you thinking of harming yourself?" is best.

A is incorrect because, although the nurse should remain non-judgmental, it is the nurse's responsibility to communicate directly with the patient. Giving the patient a pamphlet is a more passive form of communication than a direct face-to-face discussion. Offering written material does not guarantee that the patient will read it or that the patient can understand it.

B is incorrect because observing for behavioral cues may be an important nursing assessment, but it is not as useful as direct questioning.

D is incorrect because the nurse should remain focused on the here-and-now. Determining how the patient is feeling and if the patient has ever thought about self-harm is most important. Talking about the future may demonstrate the nurse is not comfortable with the subject.

59. A patient admitted for alcohol abuse and anxiety has become angry and aggressive, striking out at another patient and hitting a staff member. The patient is taken to seclusion and administered haloperidol and lorazepam. In this scenario, the haloperidol and lorazepam are considered:

    A. Chemical restraints
    B. Medication time out
    C. False imprisonment
    D. Malpractice

Rationale:

Correct answer: A.

Medications can be classified as chemical restraints when given specifically to treat the patient's condition or diagnosis. Psychotropic drugs should not be used for discipline or staff convenience. If they are used to decrease physical aggression and prevent the patient from harming themselves or others, this is often acceptable practice, if allowed according to the facility's policy.

Inappropriate use can cause deep sedation, increased agitation, and increased combativeness.

B is incorrect because a *medication time out* is not appropriate nursing language. (This may be real-world terminology, but is not reflected in nursing textbooks.)

C is incorrect because false imprisonment is the use of restraints *without* sufficient justification. In the situation described in the question, the patient *has* already displayed violent behavior and has hit a member of the staff, so legally, the nurse *can* justify the use of restraints. Note: The smallest dose of medication should be used, and the patient should be monitored closely for adverse reactions and therapeutic effects on behavior. Another example of false imprisonment is when a patient is denied the right to leave the facility after Against Medical Advice (AMA) papers have already been signed.

D is incorrect because malpractice is professional negligence in which a nurse's action causes harm or injury to the patient. The situation in the question above cannot be defined as malpractice unless more information is given about how the chemical restraint caused harm to the patient.

60. The nurse is reviewing the chart of a patient in the inpatient psychiatric unit and notes the patient's

admission was voluntary. Which of the following types of behavior would the nurse anticipate from this patient?

A. Fearfulness regarding treatment
B. Anger and aggressiveness toward others
C. Understanding of pathology and symptoms of the diagnosis
D. Willingness to participate in planning the care and treatment plan

Rationale:

Correct answer: D.

When a patient seeks help for their diagnosis or symptoms by a voluntary admission to a psychiatric unit, they are most often willing to participate in treatment programs.

A is incorrect because the fear of treatment and mistrust of staff is more likely to be seen in patients who have been involuntarily admitted to the facility.

B is incorrect because anger and aggressiveness are not general characteristics of voluntary admission.

C is incorrect because voluntary admission does not guarantee the understanding of pathology and symptoms, only a desire for help.

61. The nurse is working with a male 46-year-old patient diagnosed with paranoid schizophrenia in the inpatient psychiatric unit. Which outcome related to this patient's delusional perceptions would be appropriate for the nurse to establish?

    A. The patient will demonstrate a realistic interpretation of daily events on the unit.
    B. The patient will perform daily hygiene and grooming independently.
    C. The patient will take all prescribed medications.
    D. The patient will admit that previous perceptions of the staff were unfounded.

Rationale:

Correct answer: A.

Paranoid schizophrenia is a type of schizophrenia with a later onset in life and is not commonly seen in childhood, adolescence, or early adulthood. The patient often has distorted perceptions and is suspicious of people, facilities, and the environment plotting against him. Behavior may be angry or hostile, and the patient may experience hallucinations. A common nursing diagnosis is disturbed thought processes. The desired outcome for this patient is a realistic interpretation of daily events.

B is incorrect because, although a patient with paranoid schizophrenia may have a self-care deficit, appropriate hygiene and grooming is not a direct outcome related to delusional perceptions.

C is incorrect because, it may be appropriate, but taking medications does not relate to patient perceptions or demonstrate an improvement in thought processes.

D is incorrect because, when caring for a patient with paranoid schizophrenia, it is not necessary to discuss previous delusional or negative thought processes. The nurse should focus on reality, the here-and-now, and reassure the patient. Discussion of previous behavior can cause the patient to regress to suspicious thinking.

62. The nurse on the inpatient psychiatric unit is observing a patient admitted yesterday. The patient is insensitive to other patients, is verbally abusive, and lacks remorse. Which of the following personality disorders is the patient displaying characteristics of?

    A. Narcissistic
    B. Paranoid
    C. Histrionic
    D. Antisocial

Rationale:

Correct answer: D.

Antisocial personality disorder, or sociopathy, is characterized by a pattern of disregard for others. These patients often have a history of crime, legal problems, and aggressive or impulsive behavior. Other behaviors include a lack of a sense of guilt, immaturity, irresponsibility, promiscuous behavior, lying, cheating, and theft of others' personal belongings.

A is incorrect because narcissistic personality disorder is characterized by the need for admiration from others and grandiosity. The narcissistic patient may appear arrogant, indifferent to the disapproval of others, and have a sense of entitlement.

B is incorrect because paranoid personality disorder is characterized by patterns of distrust, suspiciousness, and interpreting the motives of others as threatening.

C is incorrect because histrionic personality disorder is characterized by excessive emotionality and attention-seeking behavior. The histrionic patient may be overreactive and show outbursts of emotion and anger.

63. The mental health nurse supervisor is working with a newly hired psychiatric nurse on the inpatient psychiatric unit. Which of the following statements by the new nurse demonstrates an understanding of when the termination

phase of the nurse-patient relationship should be discussed with the patient?

A. "On the day of scheduled discharge, I will discuss termination with the patient. We will discuss the time that was spent here and the coping skills that have been learned."
B. "After admission, before expectations are discussed, I will explain the termination phase."
C. "The nurse-patient relationship is divided into three phases: orientation, working, and termination."
D. "On the day of admission, after discussing reasons for the patient's admission and creating the plan of care, we will also discuss the discharge process and what to expect at that time."

Rationale:

Correct answer: D.

All three phases of the nurse-patient relationship should be discussed at the time of admission, so the patient understands what to expect from the relationship. It is important to build a trusting relationship from the beginning, but to also set realistic limits so the patient understands that the relationship with the nurse will end at the time of discharge.

Note: The nurse-patient relationship is divided into three phases: orientation (establishing rapport, developing a therapeutic environment), working (the exploration of client's behavior, identification of coping skills), and termination. The termination phase of the nurse-patient relationship includes evaluating patient performance, evaluating achievement of outcomes, planning for future needs, making referrals, and dealing with common behaviors associated with termination.

A is incorrect because the nurse should not wait to discuss the termination phase until the time of discharge because this can be alarming to the patient.

B is incorrect because when admitting the patient, the nurse should first develop rapport, then discuss the plan of care (including expectations), and then inform the patent about the termination phase.

C is incorrect because it is a true statement, but it does not demonstrate that the new nurse understands *when* the termination phase should be discussed.

64. The nurse is working with a patient in the crisis intervention group. The nurse considers a response to crisis intervention successful if the patient:

    A. Changes their coping skills and patterns of behavior.
    B. Develops insight into why a crisis occurred.

C. Learns better how to relate to others.

D. Returns to previous levels of functioning.

Rationale:

Correct answer: D.

A crisis is a temporary state of disequilibrium, of disturbance in homeostasis precipitated by a specific physical or psychosocial traumatic event. Crisis intervention is based on focusing on the here-and-now, encouraging verbalization of feelings, resolving emotional responses. The main goals of crisis intervention are to assist patients in returning to a previous level of functioning and to equip the patient with adaptive coping mechanisms.

A is incorrect because *changing* coping skills and patterns of behavior is not the primary outcome of crisis intervention. In some instances, a patient may substitute one unhealthy coping mechanism for another which is not necessarily a positive outcome.

B is incorrect because determining the cause of the event and figuring out why a crisis occurred is a part of crisis intervention but not the primary outcome.

C is incorrect because learning how to relate to others is a benefit and is a generally good outcome but not the primary outcome of crisis intervention.

65. A patient admitted voluntarily for anxiety disorder is demanding release from the inpatient psychiatric unit. What is the first action the nurse should take?

   A. Contact the healthcare provider.
   B. Call the family to arrange transportation.
   C. Persuade the patient to stay a few more days.
   D. Inform the patient that leaving may result in involuntary commitment.

Rationale:

Correct answer: A.

Patients who admit themselves voluntarily have the right to demand and obtain release. The nurse should be familiar with policies and procedures for admission and discharge. The first action the nurse should take is to contact the healthcare provider who can evaluate the patient and discuss discharge.

B is incorrect because arranging transportation is appropriate, but physical care of the patient takes priority. The healthcare provider should be called immediately to evaluate the patient and determine if it is safe to allow the patient to leave the facility. If the patient is unstable, AMA papers will need to be signed before the patient is released.

C is incorrect because the patient has the right to leave and persuasion is non-therapeutic.

D is incorrect because the nurse should not threaten the patient.

66. The psychiatric unit nurse is interviewing a patient admitted today who was raped one week ago. When the nurse asks about the rape, the patient becomes anxious and starts crying. What is the best intervention by the nurse?

    A. Encourage the patient to talk about the rape so the information can be documented.
    B. Acknowledge the patient's feelings and tell her the discussion can take place when she is ready.
    C. Give the patient privacy and return to discuss the situation when the patient is less anxious.
    D. Remind the patient that everything said is confidential.

Rationale:

Correct answer: B.

The acute psychological response to rape may last 2-4 weeks. This patient is still in the initial stages of reacting to the crisis, and an assessment should be performed when the patient is expressing minimal anxiety. Any discussion that induces distress should be postponed to another time.

A is incorrect because pushing for information that induces anxiety does not help the patient. All information about nursing care and the patient's response *should* be documented in the chart, but documentation is not the greatest nursing priority.

C is incorrect since the nurse should not leave the patient alone. The nurse can use therapeutic silence as a way to show compassion and build trust and discuss the situation at a later time.

D is incorrect because it does not address the patient's current anxiety. This may also give false reassurance, because some information may need to be shared with law enforcement.

67. A patient in the inpatient psychiatric unit tells the nurse, "Everyone would be better off if I wasn't alive." Which of the following nursing diagnoses would the nurse assign to this patient?

　　A. Disturbed thought process
　　B. Ineffective coping
　　C. Risk for self-harm
　　D. Impaired social interaction

Rationale:

Correct answer: C.

Any patient statements that indicate suicidal thoughts should be taken seriously by the nurse and the patient should be further assessed for risk factors. The nurse should communicate using direct questions when caring for a potentially suicidal patient. One-thought sentences and direct yes/no questions about thoughts of self-harm are appropriate for this patient assessment.

A is incorrect because the nursing diagnosis of disturbed thought process does not address the patient's statement and its seriousness.

B is incorrect because ineffective coping may be an additional nursing diagnosis for this patient, but the risk for self-harm is the diagnosis that is more specifically reflected by the patient's statement.

D is incorrect because the patient's statement does not necessarily reflect impaired social interaction. (Without more information, the nurse does not know that the patient's feelings are, indeed, founded on his own personal social interactions.)

68. The nurse is interviewing a 16-year-old patient who confides he wants to kill a peer on the football team. When

he asks the nurse if it can be a secret, what is the best response by the nurse?

- A. "I can keep your secret for now but we need to discuss how to deal with your emotions so you can avoid committing a crime."
- B. "I am required to keep your information confidential."
- C. "This information needs to be shared with your treatment team and your parents."
- D. "I won't tell your parents, but I have to share this with your treatment team."

Rationale:

Correct answer: C.

Intent to harm another individual or to break the law must be reported to the nursing supervisor. This information will be shared with the parents of a minor and the healthcare team. The threat to injure another person, along with sexual abuse, suicide, and any issues that place the patient or someone else at risk, cannot necessarily be kept a secret by the nurse. It is important for the nurse to communicate this clearly with the patient so that the nurse-patient relationship is not jeopardized and to protect the nurse's license. Failure to report can result in legal action against both the nurse and the facility.

A is incorrect because the nurse must report the information that has been shared.

B is incorrect because, generally, patient information must be kept confidential, but when the nurse knows of an intent to kill or harm someone else, it must be reported to the nursing supervisor.

D is incorrect because this information must be shared with the supervisor, the parents, and the treatment team.

69. The nurse is reviewing the chart of a patient who was just admitted to the inpatient psychiatric unit involuntarily. Which intervention should the nurse implement for this patient?

    A. Monitor the patient closely for risk of harm to self and others.
    B. Assist in completing the application for admission.
    C. Give the patient written information regarding the diagnosed mental illness.
    D. Discuss with the family why they believed the admission was needed.

Rationale:

Correct answer: A.

Involuntary admission is used when a person is at risk of harming themselves or others. This is done regardless of the patient's consent to hospitalization.

B is incorrect because an application for admission is not used with involuntary admission.

C is incorrect because written information is not appropriate at this time. When the patient is involuntarily admitted, the diagnosis may not be clear. When communication about a diagnosis is appropriate, direct teaching by the nurse is more effective than written materials.

D is incorrect because the family may or may not have had a role in admitting the patient. An assessment of reasons for admission does not take priority over monitoring for harmful behaviors and assuring patient safety.

70. The nurse is conducting an assessment interview on a 25-year-old male patient being admitted for bipolar disorder. When the patient asks why the assessment needs to be done, what is the best response by the nurse?

    A. "In order to help you in the best way possible, I need to tell your doctor about you and how you think."
    B. "This interview is an opportunity for you to express your feelings."

C. "I need to know details about your past so we can find out why you have these mental health issues."

D. "This will help us form a relationship where we can work together to discuss problems, goals, and plans for your treatment."

Rationale:

Correct answer: D.

The assessment interview is completed to establish rapport with the patient, learn more about the issues he is presenting, and work on creating goals and plans for treatment.

A is incorrect because it does not establish rapport with the patient. This statement focuses on the doctor, but the nurse should remain focused on the nurse-patient relationship.

B is incorrect, because, although the assessment interview *does* provide an opportunity to express feelings, that is not the main goal. When the patient asks a question, it is the nurse's responsibility to respond with factual information that the patient can understand.

C is incorrect because it does not foster a mutual relationship or establish rapport with the patient. It is not the nurse's responsibility to determine *why* the patient has mental health issues. The nurse's focus is to collect information, establish a trusting relationship, and provide safe nursing care according to the care plan and the healthcare provider's orders.

71. A 32-year-old female patient recently diagnosed with breast cancer is pacing the floor, has rapid speech, complains of a headache, and can hear the nurse, but is having trouble focusing. The nurse would assess this level of anxiety as:

    A. Mild
    B. Moderate
    C. Severe
    D. Panic

Rationale:

Correct answer: C.

This patient is displaying severe anxiety as evidenced by pacing, rapid speech, headaches, and an inability to focus.

A is incorrect because mild anxiety is characterized by mild muscle tension, fidgeting, a high degree of alertness. But also, a retained concentration and problem-solving ability.

B is incorrect because moderate anxiety is characterized by moderate muscle tension, periodic pacing, an increased rate of speech, and some difficulty in concentration.

D is incorrect because panic is characterized by immobilization, incoherence, feeling overwhelmed, and disorganization. The patient in panic may also not be able to see or hear and may show regression.

72. A patient in the mental health clinic is talking with the nurse about his depression. He tells the nurse he has always been a practicing Mormon but recently he has questioned his beliefs. Which of the following nursing diagnoses best fits the patient's comment?

   A. Risk for self-harm
   B. Readiness for enhanced religiosity
   C. Spiritual distress
   D. Moral distress

Rationale:

Correct answer: C.

The patient is expressing distress regarding religion and his spiritual well-being. One of the defining characteristics of the NANDA diagnosis, Spiritual Distress, is expressing concern or doubt in one's belief system.

A is incorrect because the patient is not expressing anything that specifies the risk for self-harm. The nurse should be careful not to make assumptions that a patient who questions his belief system is at risk for harming himself or others.

B is incorrect because readiness for enhanced religiosity is an actual NANDA diagnosis, but it is not indicated by the patient's statement. Characteristics for this diagnosis include the interest and ability to increase reliance on religious beliefs and/or participate in rituals of a particular faith tradition. The patient described in this question is not exhibiting a willingness to learn more or increase participation in religious activities.

D is incorrect because the patient's statement does not reflect his thoughts about moral issues. The issue the patient is expressing is one of the religious beliefs.

73. A 24-year-old man is brought to the emergency room in an incoherent, psychotic state. The patient's friend is with him and offers to share information. Which response by the nurse is appropriate?

   A. "That would violate patient confidentiality laws, I'm sorry."
   B. "I will call his healthcare provider so we can get the information that way."
   C. "Any information you could share regarding his history would be very helpful."

D. "Yes, but we will need to get a signed release from him for the information."

Rationale:

Correct answer: C.

Due to the fact that this patient is unable to provide any information or history, the friend is considered a secondary source of information. This will help the treatment team identify the issue and begin treating him immediately. The nurse's primary focus is immediate, safe patient care.

A is incorrect because obtaining information from a secondary source is not prohibited by confidentiality laws. The patient is unable to provide personal information due to their current physical state, so the information must be obtained from whoever is there at the time of admission.

B is incorrect because the patient needs to be treated immediately, and the friend is a source of information of events leading up to the emergency room visit. It is within the nurse's scope of practice to gather important information that might help the patient. Waiting for the healthcare provider to arrive to perform the interview may delay patient care.

D is incorrect because this patient is incompetent to sign a release (which is not necessary for a secondary source of information upon admission.) A signed release may be necessary to *give out* information to someone who is not a family member.

74. The student nurse is learning about medications used in the inpatient psychiatric unit. Which of the following statements about medications is incorrect?

    A. "Fluoxetine is an antidepressant and can act as a stimulant, increasing motivation."
    B. "Diazepam is a benzodiazepine which can be used for anxiety, but should be avoided in any patients experiencing withdrawal from alcohol."
    C. "Risperidone is an antipsychotic medication. Patients taking this medication should be monitored for orthostatic hypotension."
    D. "Patients taking lithium for bipolar should increase their dietary salt intake."

Rationale:

Correct answer: B.

Diazepam is a benzodiazepine that can be used to treat anxiety and seizures. It can also be used for sedation. Diazepam is safe to use and is often used in patients experiencing alcohol withdrawal.

A is incorrect because it is a true statement. Fluoxetine is a selective serotonin reuptake inhibitor (SSRI) antidepressant prescribed for major depressive disorder.

C is incorrect because it is a correct statement. Risperidone is an atypical antipsychotic medication, often used to treat schizophrenia. Adverse reactions include sedation, orthostatic hypotension, and rarely, tardive dyskinesia.

D is incorrect because it is a true statement. Lithium is an antimanic medication that can cause fluid and sodium loss, so patients should be encouraged to increase sodium in the diet and drink more than 2.5 liters of PO fluid daily to prevent dehydration.

75. A patient is upset and crying after telling the nurse about his father's recent, sudden death. Which of the following responses by the nurse demonstrates empathy?

    A. "I'm so sorry. My father died three years ago, so I understand your feelings."
    B. "You need to focus on you now. Take time for yourself."
    C. "This must be difficult to deal with."
    D. "I know you will move on after this, it just takes time."

Rationale:

Correct answer: C.

The nurse is demonstrating empathy with this statement because it reflects an understanding of what this patient is feeling. Principles of therapeutic communication include restating, reflecting, encouraging discussion of feelings, therapeutic silence, promoting clarification and insight, communication of understanding and acceptance, and identification of problems.

A is incorrect because the statement focuses on the nurse. The nurse should avoid I-statements, when possible, to keep the focus on the patient.

B is incorrect because telling the patient to focus on themselves does not address the patient's feelings. Changing the subject is not a therapeutic communication technique. The patient should be encouraged to verbalize feelings.

D is incorrect because telling the patient he will move on is closed-ended and not empathetic. This offers false reassurance and does not provide validation for how the patient is feeling.

76. A patient in the community mental health clinic tells the nurse he is afraid of elevators and avoids riding in them. He tells the nurse he fears he will die inside, and this has

affected his ability to focus on his studies in college. The nurse considers this patient is suffering from which of the following?

A. Agoraphobia
B. Social phobia
C. Claustrophobia
D. Xenophobia

Rationale:

Correct answer: C.

This patient is suffering from claustrophobia, which is the fear of closed spaces. Appropriate nursing care for the patient experiencing a phobia includes: avoiding confrontation, not humiliating the patient, encouraging relaxation, use of an unhurried approach, and encouraging exercise, activities, and hobbies.

A is incorrect because agoraphobia is the fear of open spaces.

B is incorrect because a social phobia is a fear of performing with others present, which can be humiliating or embarrassing.

D is incorrect because xenophobia is the fear of strangers.

77. The initial intervention for a patient who suffers from claustrophobia should be which of the following?

A. Encourage verbalizing fears.
B. Assist him in finding related meaning to his past.
C. Reassure the patient that he does not need to be afraid of any closed spaces on the unit.
D. Accept the patient's fears without criticizing.

Rationale:

Correct answer: D.

Patients with claustrophobia usually know their fear is irrational, but are unable to control their fear. The initial intervention by the nurse is to be accepting and nonjudgmental.

A is incorrect because encouraging verbalizing fears is appropriate, but the trusting nurse-patient relationship should be developed *first*. This is done by showing acceptance and maintaining a non-critical approach.

B is incorrect because finding related meaning is appropriate, and may be covered in a later therapy session, but this is not the initial nursing intervention.

C is incorrect, because, when a patient has a phobia, it is not helpful for the nurse to focus initially on reducing the fear.

78. A female patient has a history of incarceration for physically abusing her partner. She is admitted to the

inpatient psychiatric unit after making suicidal threats. When talking with the nurse, she expresses remorse over her past actions. Which of the following responses by the nurse is most therapeutic?

- A. "Feeling guilt is actually good, it means we can help you."
- B. "Feeling guilt is normal. What you did was terrible, but it's in the past. Let's focus on getting better."
- C. "Do you think you are at risk for hurting someone else?"
- D. "You feel guilt for what happened. Let's discuss some goals for us to work on that will make you desire to keep going and not hurt yourself."

Rationale:

Correct answer: D.

This answer choice uses restatement, a therapeutic communication technique that validates the patient's feelings by paraphrasing, indicating the nurse understands what the patient has expressed. Offering to work on goals with the patient will assist with establishing and maintaining a therapeutic-working relationship. It is most effective for the nurse to leave his/her own value systems behind and avoid judging patients for their thoughts, feelings, and behaviors.

A is incorrect because the nurse should avoid judgmental comments about the patient's feelings.

B is incorrect because telling the patient what she did was *terrible* is judgmental.

C is incorrect because it focuses on others. This patient has been admitted for suicidal threats, so, at this time, the nurse should remain focused on the safety of this patient, not others.

79. The nurse is interviewing a patient in the mental health community center and observing his verbal and nonverbal communication. Which of the following is true?

    A. Verbal communication is more accurate than nonverbal.
    B. Nonverbal communication is 25% of communication, while verbal communication is 75%.
    C. Nonverbal and verbal communication do not always match.
    D. Verbal communication is always straightforward, and nonverbal communication is not always congruent with one's thoughts.

    Rationale:

Correct answer: C.

Nonverbal and verbal communication do not always match. It is the nurse's responsibility to pay attention to nonverbal cues in order to get an accurate message from the patient.

A is incorrect because nonverbal is usually *more* accurate than verbal communication.

B is incorrect because nonverbal is 90% and verbal is 10% of all communication.

D is incorrect because nonverbal is usually more congruent with one's thoughts than verbal communication.

80. A patient is referred to Alcoholics Anonymous for a 20-year history of alcohol abuse. The nurse explains to a patient that the primary function of Alcoholics Anonymous is which of the following?

    A. Encourage a 10-step program.
    B. Help members maintain sobriety.
    C. Provide fellowship among members and teach positive coping mechanisms.
    D. Provide urine test kits to keep members accountable.

Rationale:

Correct answer: B.

The primary function of Alcoholics Anonymous is to help its members achieve and maintain sobriety from alcohol, one day at a time. Peer relationships are encouraged, and members learn to substitute healthy relationships and behaviors in place of alcohol consumption.

A is incorrect because Alcoholics Anonymous uses the 12-step program, but it is not the primary function.

C is incorrect because Alcoholics Anonymous does provide fellowship and teach positive coping mechanisms, but these are not the primary functions.

D is incorrect because urine test kits are not regularly provided by Alcoholics Anonymous groups.

81. The nurse in the inpatient psychiatric unit is caring for a patient with borderline personality disorder. The nurse knows the plan of care for this patient should include which of the following?

    A. Scheduled flexibility.
    B. Give medications to prevent aggression.
    C. Restrict the patient from seeing other patients.
    D. Ensure the patient follows certain restrictions.

Rationale:

Correct answer: D.

Borderline personality disorder is characterized by unstable behavior and relationships with others. This usually begins in early adulthood and is associated with depression, substance abuse, and eating disorders. These patients can be impulsive and manipulative, so the patient should be informed of policies, rules, and expectations upon admission.

A is incorrect because limits should be firm and implemented consistently.

B is incorrect because there is not a medication specific for borderline personality disorder. The nurse should use least-restrictive measures first, which includes avoiding antipsychotic medications, when possible.

C is incorrect because interactions with other patients should be allowed, but monitored, to prevent manipulation. (Keeping the borderline patient secluded from other patients prevents the patient from having opportunities for positive interaction.)

82. The nurse is speaking with a patient in the mental health community center who is agitated. His arms are crossed, and he is rapidly bouncing on his left leg. When the patient tells the nurse he's fine, which of the following responses by the nurse is therapeutic?

A. "Ok, be careful, and come get me if you feel the need to talk."
B. "If you're fine, why are you bouncing on one leg?"
C. "It appears like you are feeling something other than what you're saying. Could you tell me what's bothering you?"
D. "I find it hard to believe that. I don't think you're telling the truth."

Rationale:

Correct answer: C.

The nurse has identified an incongruence between the patient's verbal and nonverbal communication. Pointing out the discrepancy and asking for clarification is therapeutic. This is an appropriate way to assess the patient without asking, "why?".

A is incorrect because it dismisses the patient's distress. Telling the patient to "be careful" does not adequately provide for patient safety. (The patient is agitated in the mental health center; the nurse should not rely on the patient's ability to keep himself safe.)

B is incorrect because asking "why" is non-therapeutic and this may cause the patient to feel like he needs to defend himself.

D is incorrect because it is confrontational.

83. A patient diagnosed with major depression with a history of a recent suicide attempt tells the nurse, "I should have died. I'm a failure. Nothing ever goes right." Which of the following responses by the nurse is therapeutic?

   A. "You have everything to live for."
   B. "Why do you think you're a failure?"
   C. "These feelings are a normal part of depression. We can help you feel better."
   D. "Have you been feeling like a failure for a while?"

Rationale:

Correct answer: D.

This type of response to patient feelings is therapeutic. This is the technique of restating, in which the nurse acknowledges the patient's feelings of hopelessness and will allow for more open communication with the patient.

A is incorrect because the nurse's statement minimizes what the patient experienced. This is a real-world response, but is closed-ended and does not facilitate exploration of feelings.

B is incorrect because asking "why" is non-therapeutic.

C is incorrect because it blocks communication. Minimizing the patient's feelings does not facilitate an exploration of feelings.

84. The nurse is preparing to perform the admission interview of a patient on the inpatient psychiatric unit. The nurse sits close to the patient and leans in to hear the patient speak. The patient abruptly becomes frustrated and leaves the room. To what does the nurse contribute the patient's behavior?

    A. The violation of personal space.
    B. Their issues with sharing personal information.
    C. The patient is uncomfortable due to not knowing the purpose of the interview.
    D. Voices in the patient's head told the patient to leave.

Rationale:

Correct answer: A.

People respond to an invasion of personal space in different ways. Some patients may physically retreat, others may withdraw inwardly, or even respond with aggression. Sitting too close to the patient can interfere with the patient's personal space, making the patient uncomfortable. This behavior should help the nurse recognize that social distance is more appropriate for performing the admission interview of this patient.

B is incorrect because the patient has not yet shared any personal information.

C is incorrect because there is not enough evidence to come to this conclusion.

D is incorrect because there is no evidence that the patient is experiencing auditory hallucinations. The nurse should not jump to conclusions.

85. A 40-year-old patient admitted for anxiety asks the nurse what *stressors* are. What is the best response by the nurse?

    A. "Stressors are events, situations or individuals that can threaten current functioning, requiring adaptation."
    B. "Stressors are complicated stimuli in the brain that can contribute to mental illness."
    C. "The complete answer would come from your healthcare provider."
    D. "Let's not focus on stressors, let's discuss your coping skills."

Rationale:

Correct answer: A.

Stressors are external mechanisms (not necessarily personal physical health problems) that can disrupt a patient's current level of functioning. Examples of stressors can include children, spouse, parents, health problems of family members, individuals, job expectations, lifestyle, body image, finances, and situational role changes. Stressors require some form of coping or adaptation and sometimes a formation of new coping mechanisms. This can be difficult for patients with mental illness and anxiety who are already dealing with their own health as a source of personal stress.

B is incorrect because stressors external factors, not stimuli in the brain.

C is incorrect because this statement passes the buck by abdicating patient education to the healthcare provider. The nurse should respond to the patient's question within the nurse's knowledge before calling the healthcare provider.

D is incorrect because, although discussing coping skills may be helpful, it does not address the patient's question.

86. A patient is in the community mental health center discussing a friend's recent suicide. When the patient asks the nurse for suggestions to cope with the stress, what is the best response by the nurse?

    A. "You should spend some time alone to reflect and avoid explaining your feelings repetitively."
    B. "We could talk to the healthcare provider about antianxiety medication."

C. "What hobbies are you interested in that might get your mind off of it?"

D. "We have a loss support group you can attend, and you are also encouraged to talk with your friends about your loss."

Rationale:

Correct answer: D.

Social support and support groups are effective ways the nurse could suggest for helping the patient cope with the stress of losing a friend to suicide.

A is incorrect because isolation is not recommended for someone in emotional distress. The nurse should not dismiss the opportunity to show emotional support to a patient expressing anguish.

B is incorrect since the patient is not displaying signs of anxiety. Before recommending medication, the nurse should first attempt therapeutic communication techniques, build a trusting relationship, and encourage expression of feelings.

C is incorrect because distraction is only a temporary coping measure. The patient is showing readiness to learn to cope at this time, so the nurse should not postpone learning by suggesting hobbies.

87. Cultural factors and other protective factors can influence suicide rates in many areas of the world. Which of the following are true regarding these factors related to suicide?

    A. American Indians and Pacific Islanders have the lowest rates of suicide.
    B. Religion is a protective factor for Hispanic Americans.
    C. Asian Americans have the highest rates of suicide.
    D. Older African American women have the highest risk for suicide.

Rationale:

Correct answer: B.

Most Hispanic Americans practice Roman Catholicism. In this religion, suicide is considered a sin, preventing the individual from going to Heaven. Thus, this is a protective factor, reducing the rate of suicide within this cultural group.

A is incorrect because American Indians and Pacific Islanders have the highest rates of suicide.

C is incorrect because Asian Americans have the lowest rates of suicide.

D is incorrect because older African American women have a low risk for suicide.

88. The nurse is interviewing a patient in the inpatient psychiatric unit. When the patient tells the nurse he only uses alcohol and cocaine because of his stressful marriage and increasingly difficult job, which defense mechanism is the patient using?

    A. Displacement
    B. Projection
    C. Rationalization
    D. Sublimation

Rationale:

Correct answer: C.

Rationalization is the use of excuses for maladaptive behavior. This patient is defending his use of alcohol and cocaine by relating it to life stressors, which is a common defense mechanism in patients who abuse substances.

A is incorrect because displacement is the transference of emotions to achieve a decrease in a patient's anxiety.

B is incorrect because projection is defending oneself by denying the existence of qualities and attributing those qualities to another individual.

D is incorrect because sublimation is unconsciously transforming socially unacceptable impulses into acceptable ones.

89. The nurse is meeting with a patient admitted to the inpatient psychiatric unit for anorexia nervosa. The nurse knows the patient is improving if which of the following occurs?

    A. She willingly attends mealtime in the patient dining room.
    B. She has adequate fluid intake and gains 4-5 pounds in a week.
    C. She attends unit activities with other patients.
    D. She gains 1-2 pounds in a week.

Rationale:

Correct answer: D.

Weight gain is the best indication of a patient's improvement with anorexia nervosa. The goal is 1-2 pounds gained per week. The patient should be monitored during mealtimes and the nurse should make accurate documentation of amounts of foods ingested. The patient should be monitored closely after mealtimes to be sure she is not purging after meals.

A is incorrect because her presence in the dining room during mealtime does not equate to the patient's nutritional intake. The patient may attend mealtime with other patients as a way to manipulate staff into thinking that she is consuming healthy amounts of food.

B is incorrect because it is not realistic for a patient with anorexia to gain this much weight in a week. The goal is 1-2 pounds per week. Fluids are not the main concern for this patient. If the patient over-hydrates, this could lead to weight gain which is not reflective of good nutritional intake.

C is incorrect because attending unit activities shows that the patient is willing to socialize, but is not a direct indicator of improvement from anorexia.

90. The newly admitted patient diagnosed with bulimia is not in control of her eating habits. An appropriate goal the nurse will set for this patient is:

    A. The patient will learn basic problem-solving skills.
    B. The patient will have increased food intake at each meal.
    C. The patient will perform self-care daily.
    D. The patient will decrease the sweets consumed at each meal.

Rationale:

Correct answer: A.

Eating disorders are commonly a manifestation of underlying self-image issues, poor self-esteem, and an inadequate ability to adapt to stressful life situations and manage problems faced in daily life. This patient will begin to gain a sense of control over her life if basic problem-solving skills are learned.

B is incorrect because patients with bulimia often do *already* increase their food intake by binge-eating. The patent needs to learn healthy eating habits, portion control, coping strategies, and problem-solving.

C is incorrect because patients with bulimia do not commonly have a self-care deficit, and this will not improve the patient's sense of control.

D is incorrect because the patient with bulimia does not need to decrease sweets at each meal. The patient with bulimia binges and purges, so learning about adequate, balanced caloric intake with each meal is a priority. The nurse should not make the assumption that the bulimic patient eats a lot of sweets.

91. The nurse is interviewing a patient admitted with bulimia. The nurse knows the following interventions will promote a therapeutic relationship except:

A. Establishing an atmosphere of trust.
B. Discussing purging behaviors.
C. Helping to identify feelings associated with binge-purge behavior.
D. Teaching the patient about bulimia and treatment options.

Rationale:

Correct answer: B.

Patients diagnosed with bulimia are often ashamed of their eating and purging behaviors. A discussion regarding bulimia should focus on the feelings, not the behaviors themselves.

A is incorrect because establishing an atmosphere of trust promotes a therapeutic relationship. Often, the patient will not respond to treatment until she feels she can trust her nurse.

C is incorrect because helping identify feelings promotes a therapeutic relationship between the patient and the nurse.

D is incorrect because teaching the patient about bulimia and treatment modalities promote a therapeutic relationship.

92. A 24-year-old patient is admitted to the medical unit with sudden onset paralysis of both lower extremities. Tests have found no injury or reason for the paralysis. The nurse plans interventions based on which statement about conversion disorder?

   A. Symptoms are a conscious effort to control anxiety.
   B. The patient experiences high levels of anxiety due to paralysis.
   C. Physical symptoms have psychological significance.
   D. A confrontational approach can benefit the patient.

Rationale:

Correct answer: C.

Conversion disorder is a psychiatric condition in which a patient experiences the loss of sight, **paralysis**, numbness, or other neurologic symptoms for which no medical explanation can be found. The patient subconsciously experiences physical body symptoms in order to reduce psychological anxiety. In conversion disorder, the physical paralysis is significant of psychological distress.

A is incorrect because conversion disorder occurs unconsciously.

B is incorrect because the patient is not experiencing distress due to lost or altered body function. Rather, the altered body function is a result of the anxiety.

D is incorrect because confrontation is inappropriate and may aggravate the patient's anxiety.

93. A male patient on the inpatient psychiatric unit has a diagnosis of borderline personality disorder. The patient consistently breaks unit rules, and the nurse knows the behavior must be confronted because it will help the patient:

    A. Reduce euphoria
    B. Manage anxiety
    C. Set realistic goals
    D. Become more self-aware

Rationale:

Correct answer: D.

The patient with borderline personality disorder must become aware of his own behavior before being expected to change his behavior. Identification and verbalization of feelings must be encouraged. The nurse must remain empathetic and set consistent limits, offering support while enforcing facility rules.

A is incorrect because patients with borderline personality disorder don't commonly feel euphoric. If they do feel overjoyed, they aren't likely to want to suppress that feeling. These patients are often depressed, have a labile mood, and have periods of intense anger.

B is incorrect because anxiety is not a characteristic of borderline personality disorder, and confrontation is not a technique for therapeutically reducing anxiety.

C is incorrect because setting realistic goals occurs after becoming more self-aware.

94. The nurse in the mental health community center is working with patients in a support group. Which of the following, regarding social and therapeutic relationships, are true? (Select all that apply.)

    A. Both parties' needs are met in social relationships, while in therapeutic relationships, only the individual patient's needs are considered.
    B. Social relationships include advice-giving, while in therapeutic relationships, advice-giving is not therapeutic.
    C. One member's feelings and issues are explored in a social relationship, while therapeutic relationships are created for friendship.

D. Problem-solving and solutions are mutual in social relationships, while in therapeutic relationships, solutions are only implemented by the patient.

E. Communication is deep and evaluated in social relationships, while in therapeutic relationships, communication is superficial.

Rationale:

Correct answer: A, B, D.

Therapeutic relationships between nurses and patients are characterized by considering patient needs only, not giving advice, and problem-solving by the patient.

C is incorrect because therapeutic relationships are not friendships.

E is incorrect because communication in therapeutic relationships is deep and evaluated.

95. Which of the following statements are examples of therapeutic communication? (Select all that apply.)

    A. "Why weren't you in group this morning?"
    B. "It sounds like you have difficulty sleeping from what you've said."
    C. "What did your girlfriend do that made you want to leave? Did she abuse you? Are you angry?"

D. "I would quit your job, if I were you, and do something else."

E. "So, things at home are very difficult lately?"

Rationale:

Correct answer: B, E.

These statements use restating, exploring, and reflecting. These are all examples of therapeutic communication.

A is incorrect because *why* questions are not therapeutic.

C is incorrect because it involves the use of excessive questioning. Asking the patient numerous questions, in succession, can increase the patient's anxiety.

D is incorrect because giving advice is non-therapeutic.

96. A patient who was admitted voluntarily has become physically and verbally abusive while demanding discharge from the inpatient psychiatric unit. The nurse calls security and applies physical restraints to the patient. Which of the following legal ramifications are possible for this nurse? (Select all that apply.)

    A. Libel
    B. Battery
    C. Assault
    D. Slander

E. False imprisonment

Rationale:

Correct answer: B, C, E.

The nurse may be charged with false imprisonment, as leaving the hospital has been prevented, and there may not be facility policies regarding detaining the patient. Assault is offensive, unwanted contact, and battery is unintentional touching without restraint. These are restraining a patient in a situation that did not meet the criteria for the intervention.

A is incorrect because the nurse did not make untrue statements about the patient in writing.

D is incorrect because the nurse did not make untrue spoken statements about the patient.

97. The nurse is working on the inpatient psychiatric unit. The nurse knows which of the following are therapeutic communication techniques? (Select all that apply.)

    A. Restating
    B. Listening
    C. Asking "why"
    D. Using neutral responses
    E. Providing acknowledgement and feedback
    F. Providing advice and approval, or disapproval

Rationale:

Correct answer: A, B, D, E.

Therapeutic communication techniques include restating, listening, neutral responses, and providing acknowledgment and feedback. This encourages patients to share feelings and beliefs regarding their mental illness and can help patients participate in goal planning and nursing interventions.

C is incorrect because asking *why* is perceived as accusatory, and can cause patients to feel threatened, or in need to defend themselves.

F is incorrect because advice, approval, and disapproval are barriers to therapeutic nursing communication.

98. The nurse on the inpatient psychiatric unit is caring for a new patient admitted following a rape. The nurse knows the initial care of this patient should include which of the following? (Select all that apply.)

    A. Assure privacy.
    B. Use therapeutic touch with the patient to demonstrate acceptance and empathy.
    C. Accompany the patient for physical examinations.
    D. Maintain a non-judgmental approach.
    E. Encourage the patient to talk about the event.

Rationale:

Correct answer: A, C, D.

A victim of rape has the right to privacy. The patient is most likely anxious, so accompanying the patient for examinations will keep the patient safe and offer emotional support. Guilt is common after rape, and the patient should not be blamed for the event. A non-judgmental approach is best for this patient.

B is incorrect because the patient who has experienced a rape may find personal touch intrusive, so this should be avoided.

E is incorrect because the event occurred recently, and initial care would not include encouraging the patient to talk about the event until ready. The patient may need 2-4 weeks until she is ready to talk about the rape.

99. The nurse is educating the parents of a child diagnosed with ADHD about methylphenidate. The nurse tells the parents the side effects of methylphenidate include which of the following? (Select all that apply.)

    A. Anorexia
    B. Insomnia
    C. Irritability
    D. Increased attention span
    E. Constipation

Rationale:

Correct answer: A, B, C.

Side effects of methylphenidate include anorexia, insomnia, irritability, and diarrhea.

D is incorrect because increased attention span is a therapeutic effect of methylphenidate.

E is incorrect because methylphenidate is not known to cause constipation.

100. The nurse is observing violent, aggressive behavior in a patient admitted for impulse control disorder. Which of the following nursing assessment data is likely to be found? (Select all that apply.)

    A. The patient is functioning well in other areas of life.
    B. The degree of aggressiveness is not in proportion to the stressor.
    C. The violent behavior is justified by the stressor.
    D. One of the patient's parents was an alcoholic.
    E. The patient has no remorse for his lack of anger control.

Rationale:

Correct answer: A, B, D.

Patients with impulse control disorder usually function well in other areas of life. The degree of aggressiveness is out of proportion with the stressor, and there is generally a history of parental alcoholism and abuse.

C is incorrect because there is no justification for violent behavior.

E is incorrect because patients with impulse control disorder often feel remorse and guilt.

www.ingramcontent.com/pod-product-compliance
Lightning Source LLC
Chambersburg PA
CBHW062039120526
44592CB00035B/1471